From Wax to Crayon

by Avery Toolen

Bullfrog
Books

Ideas for Parents and Teachers

Bullfrog Books let children practice reading informational text at the earliest reading levels. Repetition, familiar words, and photo labels support early readers.

Before Reading

- Discuss the cover photo. What does it tell them?

- Look at the picture glossary together. Read and discuss the words.

Read the Book

- "Walk" through the book and look at the photos. Let the child ask questions. Point out the photo labels.

- Read the book to the child, or have him or her read independently.

After Reading

- Prompt the child to think more. Ask: Did you know crayons are made of wax? Have you ever thought about how crayons are made?

Bullfrog Books are published by Jump!
5357 Penn Avenue South
Minneapolis, MN 55419
www.jumplibrary.com

Library of Congress Cataloging-in-Publication Data

Names: Toolen, Avery, author.
Title: From wax to crayon / by Avery Toolen.
Description: Minneapolis, MN: Jump!, Inc., [2022]
Series: Where does it come from? | Includes index.
Audience: Ages 5–8 | Audience: Grades K–1
Identifiers: LCCN 2020047900 (print)
LCCN 2020047901 (ebook)
ISBN 9781645279884 (hardcover)
ISBN 9781645279891 (paperback)
ISBN 9781645279907 (ebook)
Subjects: LCSH: Crayons—Juvenile literature.
Paraffin wax—Juvenile literature.
Manufacturing processes—Juvenile literature.
Classification: LCC TS1268 .T66 2022 (print)
LCC TS1268 (ebook) | DDC 670—dc23
LC record available at https://lccn.loc.gov/2020047900
LC ebook record available at https://lccn.loc.gov/2020047901

Editor: Eliza Leahy
Designer: Michelle Sonnek

Photo Credits: matin/Shutterstock, cover (left); Lucie Lang/Shutterstock, cover (right), 24; RRandall/Shutterstock, 1; Studio DMM Photography/Shutterstock, 3; Sensasi/Shutterstock, 4; Chris So/Getty, 5, 23br; Bloomberg/Getty, 6–7, 22tl, 23tr; William Thomas Cain/Getty, 8–9, 10, 14–15, 16, 22tr, 22br, 23bl; GotziLA STOCK/Shutterstock, 11; Holly Kuchera/Shutterstock, 12–13, 22mr, 23tl; Stacey Newman/Shutterstock, 17; calimedia/Shutterstock, 18–19, 22bl; iStock, 20–21, 22ml.

Printed in the United States of America at Corporate Graphics in North Mankato, Minnesota.

Table of Contents

Many Colors

Ben draws with crayons.

Where do they come from?

Wax!

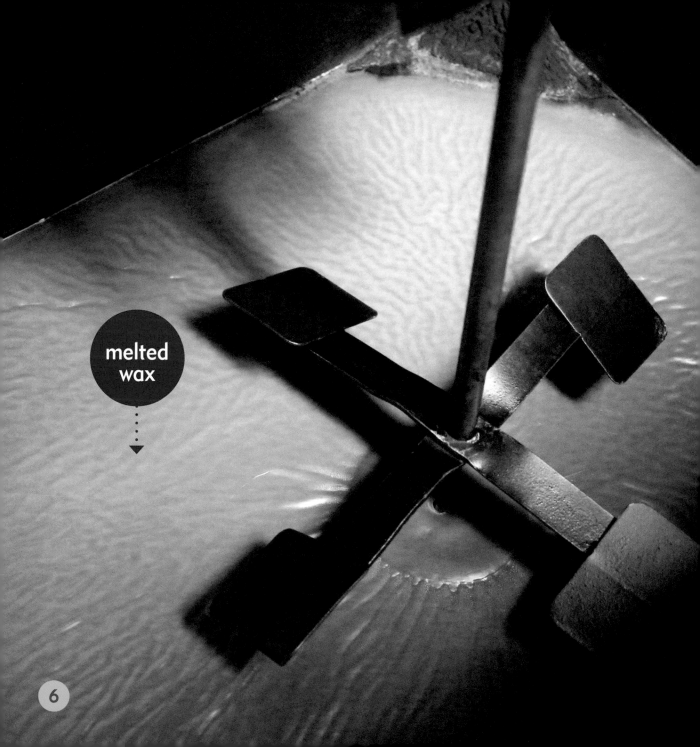

melted
wax

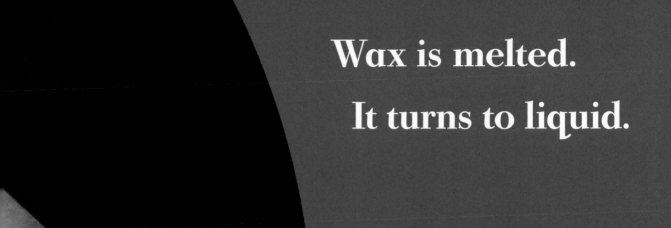

Wax is melted.
It turns to liquid.

Powder is added.
This gives the
wax color.

colored
powder

The wax goes in molds.
They shape each crayon.

mold

The wax gets hard.

A machine adds labels.

Why?

They tell us the color.

label

13

sorting machine

A machine sorts
the crayons.

How?

They are sorted
by color.

One of each color
drops down.

They go in boxes.

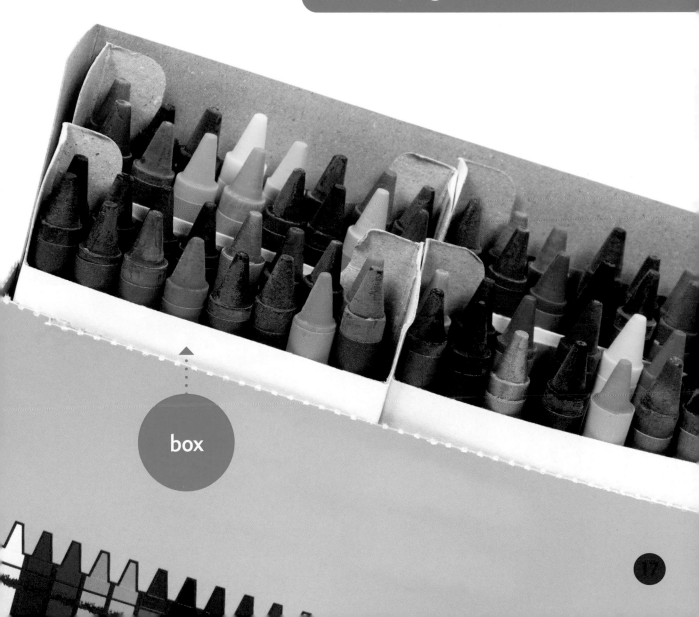

box

They go to stores.

We buy a box.

We draw.

Fun!

From Melting to Drawing

How is wax made into crayons that we use? Take a look!

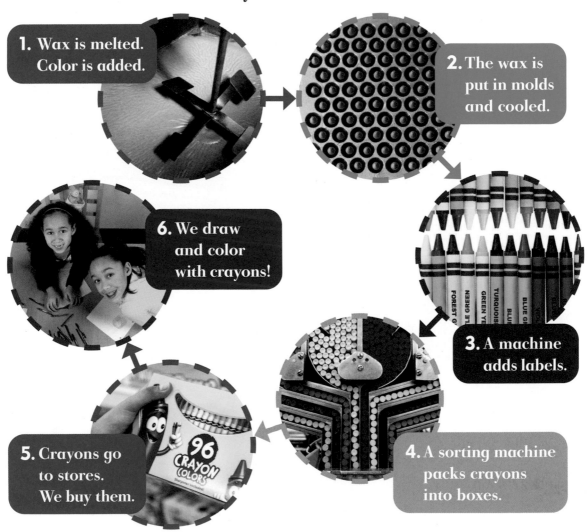

1. Wax is melted. Color is added.

2. The wax is put in molds and cooled.

3. A machine adds labels.

4. A sorting machine packs crayons into boxes.

5. Crayons go to stores. We buy them.

6. We draw and color with crayons!

96 CRAYON COLORS

Picture Glossary

labels
Materials that are attached to items to describe them.

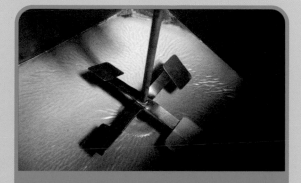

melted
Changed from a solid to a liquid, usually because of heat.

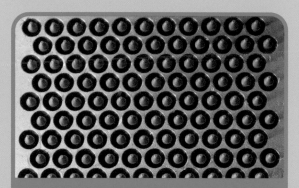

molds
Hollow forms in which things are shaped.

wax
A soft material used to make crayons, candles, and other items.

Index

To Learn More

Finding more information is as easy as 1, 2, 3.

❶ Go to www.factsurfer.com

❷ Enter "fromwaxtocrayon" into the search box.

❸ Choose your book to see a list of websites.